Simply Be More

Time preserved wisdom
through fresh eyes

Simply Be More

Time preserved wisdom
through fresh eyes

Clare Antonia Langan

Winchester, UK
Washington, USA

JOHN HUNT PUBLISHING

First published by O-Books, 2022
O-Books is an imprint of John Hunt Publishing Ltd., 3 East St., Alresford,
Hampshire SO24 9EE, UK
office@jhpbooks.com
www.johnhuntpublishing.com
www.o-books.com

For distributor details and how to order please visit the 'Ordering' section on our website.

ISBN: 978 1 78904 805 6
978 1 78904 806 3 (ebook)
Library of Congress Control Number: 2021949489

A CIP catalogue record for this book is available from the British Library.

Design: Matthew Greenfield

UK: Printed and bound by CPI Group (UK) Ltd, Croydon, CR0 4YY
Printed in North America by CPI GPS partners

We operate a distinctive and ethical publishing philosophy in
all areas of our business, from our global network of authors to
production and worldwide distribution.

Contents

Foreword

Thank you, dear reader, for picking up this book which was lovingly created just for this moment.

What you have in your hands is a creative pilgrimage born from a personal challenge to do something that I had not done since childhood, and something that would take me out of my comfort zone. I chose to do a sketch every single day for 100 days. I had not done any art to speak of since the age of thirteen. There was never the time, I was never in the right 'space' or frame of mind, the light was wrong etc., etc. In 2020 I found myself with all my work as a flute player cancelled. One thing I had in abundance was time, and as I was soon to discover, creativity.

I had recently completed writing a book called *Living Each Day the Fortune Cookie Way*, my first 'lockdown' exercise, and had sent it to a literary agent in America to be reviewed. In order to be considered, I was asked to fill in a form and to say what my second book was... Whoa! *Second book*! "There is no second book," I whispered to myself. But I had done ten sketches with accompanying words, so on a whim and using the no limits mentality that I had decided I now wanted to live my life by, I sent these ten sketches to Devra Jacobs at Dancing World Group. To my utter surprise she said, "Send these sketches to John Hunt Publishers; I have a feeling they will love the idea; there is something in it."

Once again everything in me told me that this was completely crazy but I obeyed the call and sent 14 sketches to John Hunt Publishing... The rest, as they say, is history. There were many more synchronicities along the way, but as I would discover, this is the case when you respond wholeheartedly to the creative call.

Where have the ideas come from? They have come from years

of reading self-help books and years of pursuing a spiritual life. They have been the salve that has healed me and helped me adjust to 2020. They have come out of nowhere, thin air, my runs, a dream, my morning pages... They have shown me that I am more than just my job title. They have shown me that I am being bombarded with lessons everywhere I look. In every glance the world is teaching me something if I just tune in to hear what it is saying; if I listen and look with my heart.

I hope that these images help you to hear the whisperings of your soul and prompt you to practise affirmations. The challenge to write I AM followed by something positive was huge, but as Joel Osteen says: what follows I AM becomes your reality.

You, dear reader, are complete, but do you believe it? Join me on a journey of age-old wisdom encapsulated image by image, and be brave, respond to the whisperings of your heart.

Be More Images

Just like a snail my home and I are one

a spiral of eternity within me...

Be more snail.

just like a butterfly, when I embraced change I grew my wings...

Be more butterfly.

I share my beauty and fragrance with all...

just like a rose

Be more rose.

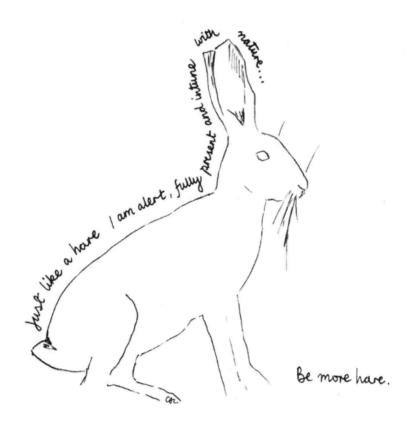

Just like a hare I am alert, fully present and intune with nature...

Be more hare.

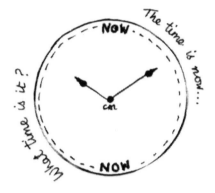

Be more now.

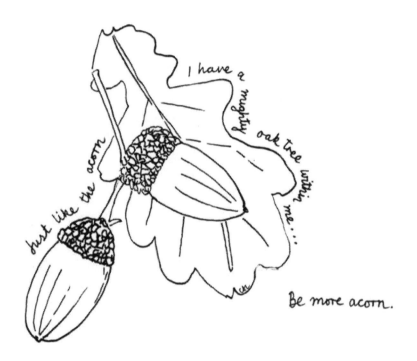

I have a mighty oak tree within me...

just like the acorn

Be more acorn.

Just like a swan I am effortlessly elegant and serene …

Be more swan.

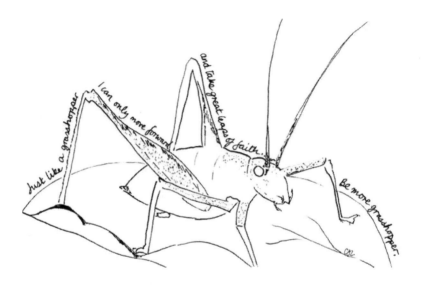

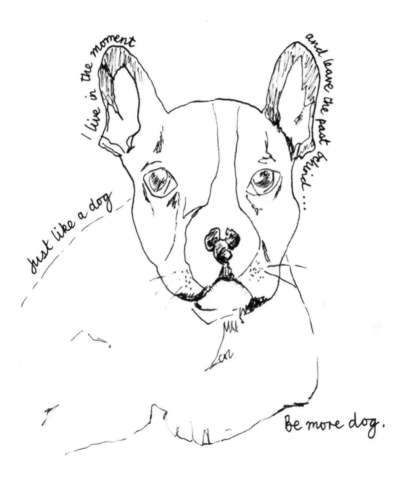

I live in the moment

and leave the past behind....

Just like a dog

Be more dog.

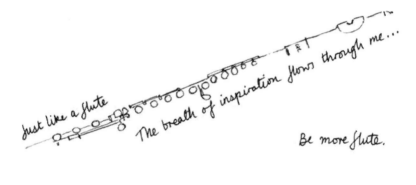

Just like a flute... The breath of inspiration flows through me...

Be more flute.

Just like a peacock

I show my true colours in all their glory...

Be more peacock

Just like a meerkat

I am playful, joyous and always alert...

Be more meerkat.

I stand tall and turn towards the light...

just like a sunflower

Be more sunflower.

I soar above the storms of life …

Just like an eagle

Be more eagle.

Just like a Queen

I reign over my world...

Be more Queer.

Just like a lion

I have great courage and strength...

Be more lion.

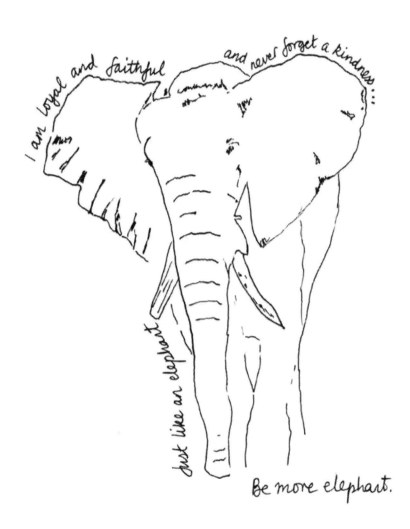

I am loyal and faithful and never forget a kindness...

Just like an elephant

Be more elephant.

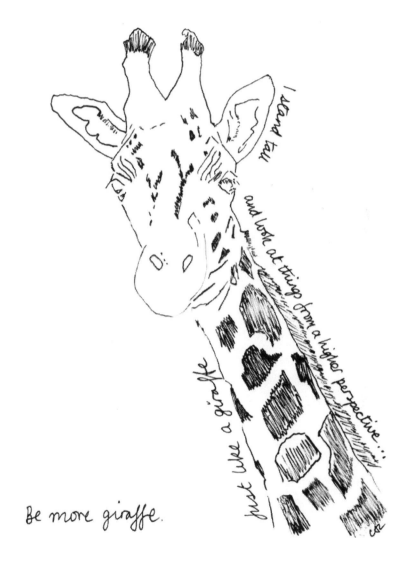

I stand tall and look at things from a higher perspective...

just like a giraffe

Be more giraffe.

I look for the sweetness in life ...

Just like a humming bird

Be more humming bird.

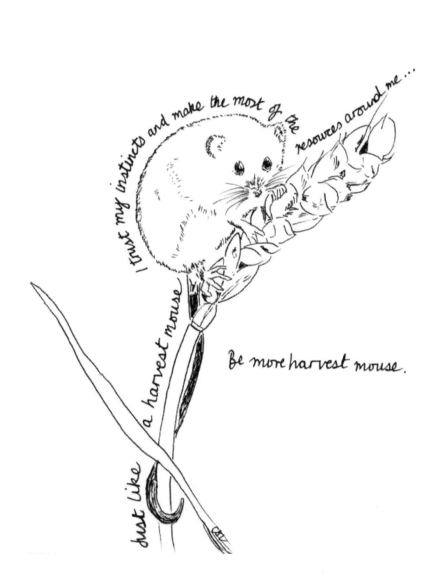

I trust my instincts and make the most of the resources around me...

Just like a harvest mouse

Be more harvest mouse.

Just like a dolphin, I am always smiling and in harmony with my surroundings.

Be more dolphin.

I make friends easily and am happy-go-lucky...

Just like Ceril the Oxford Down Ram

Be more Ceril.

just like a bee

I take time to enjoy life's nectar...

Be more bee.

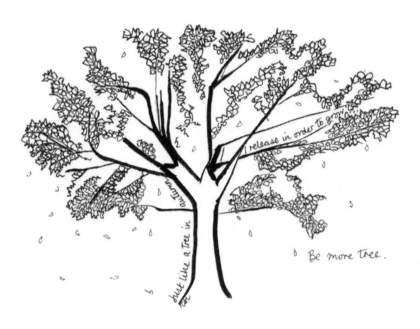

Be more tree.

Just like an owl

I see things from all perspectives …

Be more owl.

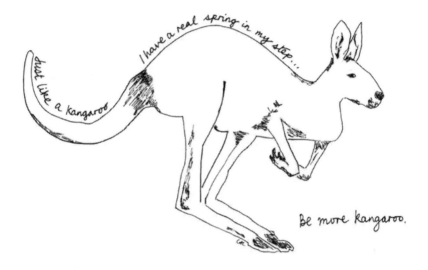

I have a real spring in my step...

Just like a kangaroo

Be more kangaroo.

Just like a tortoise I always have the option to retreat within...

Be more tortoise.

Just like a millipede I can justify every pair of shoes...

Be more millipede.

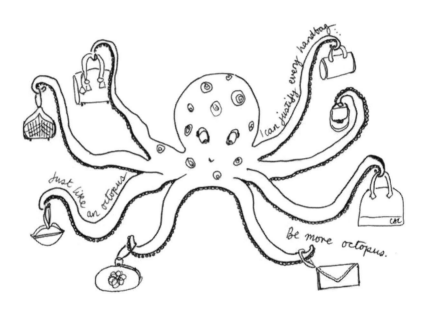

I am ready to be remoulded

and reshaped...

Be more potter.

Just like a potter

I prepare for the future...

Just like a squirrel

Be more squirrel.

Just like an angel

I radiate love...

Be more angel.

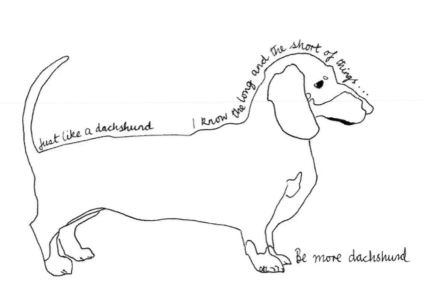

Just like a fox I have an agile mind and body...

Be more fox.

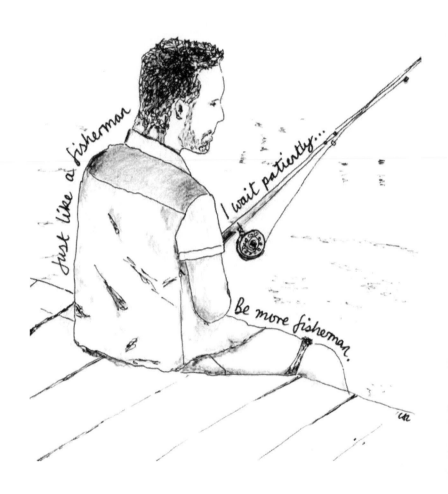

just like a fisherman

I wait patiently...

Be more fisherman.

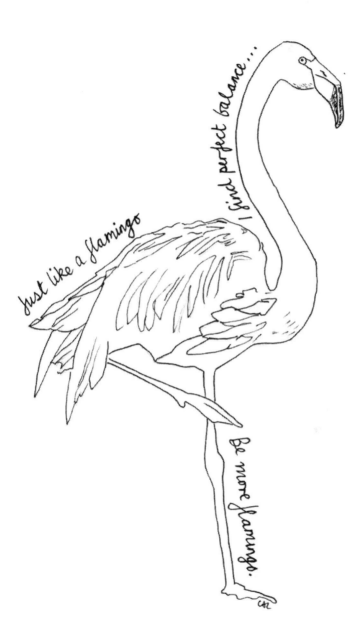

Just like a flamingo I find perfect balance...

Be more flamingo.

I make the impossible possible.

Be more magician.

Just like a magician.

Just like an alpaca

I make people smile and bring joy...

Be more alpaca.

I am mischievous and playful...

just like an emu

Be more emu.

Just like a dung beetle I take something many view as a negative and turn it into a positive...

Be more dung beetle.

just like a lotus flower. I grow out of murky waters towards the light...

Be more lotus flower.

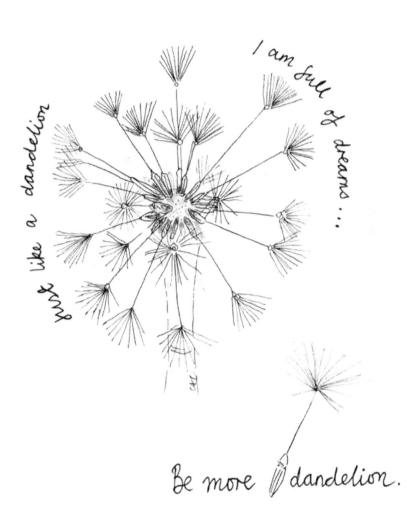

I am full of dreams ...

just like a dandelion

Be more dandelion.

Just like Shakespeare allow the creativity to flow in and through you...

Be more Shakespeare.

Just like a hedgehog sometimes it's ok to curl up in a ball...

Be more hedgehog.

just like a stag

Be the Monarch of your glen...

Be more stag.

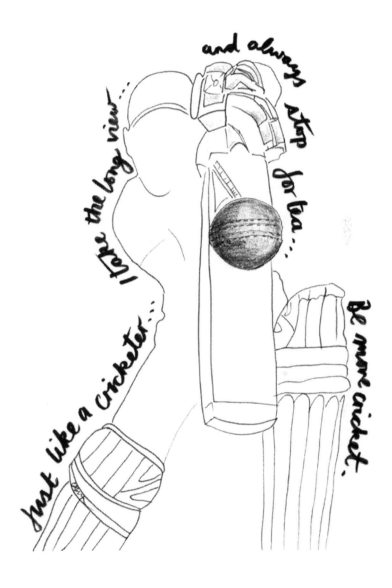

Just like a cricketer... I take the long view... and always stop for tea... Be more cricket.

just like a badger   dig deep...

Be more badger.

just like a penguin

dive deep...

 Be more penguin.

I practise

rest and relaxation...

just like a cat

Be more cat.

I am full of joie de vivre . . .

Be more french bulldog.

just like a french bulldog

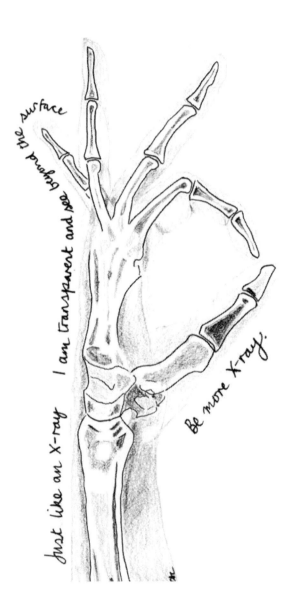

Just like an X-ray I am transparent and see beyond the surface

Be more X-ray.

Just like aries

I tackle challenges head on...

Be more aries.

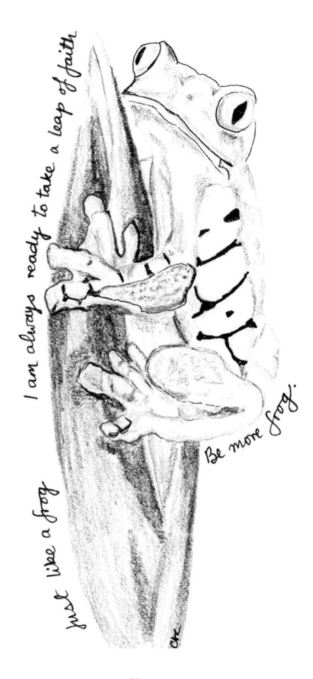

I am always ready to take a leap of faith

Be more frog.

just like a frog

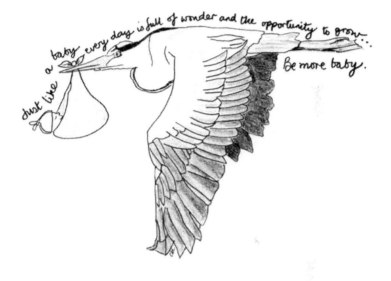

Just like a baby, every day is full of wonder and the opportunity to grow...

Be more baby.

Just like the moon

I go through different phases...

Be more moon.

Be more yogi.

I live a life of balance . . .

just like a yogi.

I stand tall and charm all who see me:

Just like a foxglove,

be more foxglove.

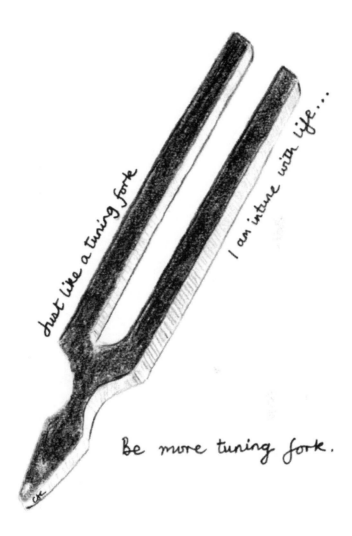

Just like a tuning fork

I am intune with life...

Be more tuning fork.

Just like a candle   I shine my light in the darkness ...

Be more candle.

I am bubbly and full of sparkles...

just like champagne

Be more
champagne

just like an oyster

the world is open to me ...

Be more oyster.

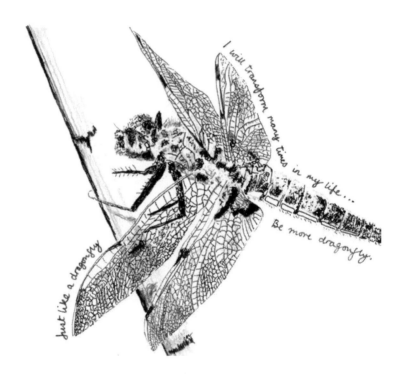

I develop my brilliance under pressure...

Be more diamond.

Just like a diamond

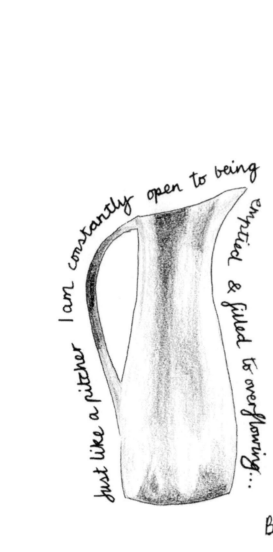

Just like a pitcher I am constantly open to being emptied & filled to overflowing...

Be more pitcher.

just like a bicycle

I am constantly evolving...

or

Be more bicycle.

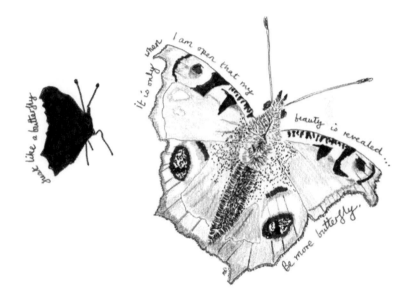

just like a butterfly

it is only when I am open that my

beauty is revealed ...

be more butterfly.

Just like an iceberg I am more unseen than seen... be more iceberg.

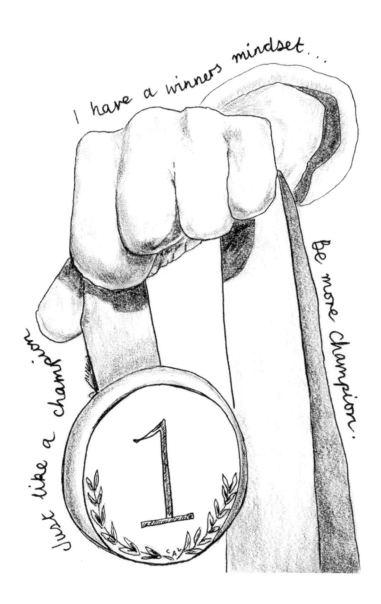

I have a winners mindset...

be more champion.

Just like a champion

reared amongst chickens

I respond to my true calling

and soar above the

...trees

just like an eagle

Be more eagle.

Just like a mosaic the broken pieces of my life make the whole ...

Be more mosaic.

I listen to my masters voice...

Be more border collie.

just like a border collie

Just like a sloth

Sometimes the best thing to do is nothing... Be more sloth

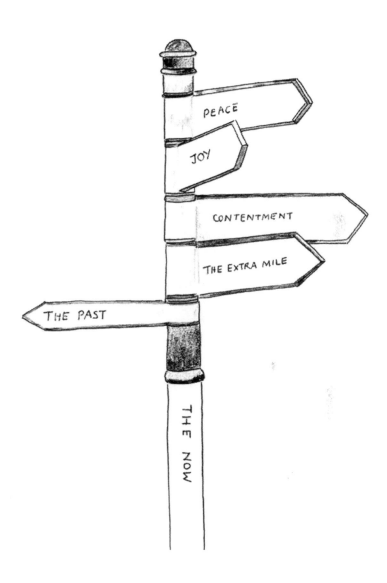

just like an author
I write the story of my life...
Be more author.

Just like a tapestry

I weave a rich design of

two sides

Be more tapestry

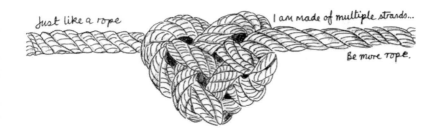

Just like a rope

I am made of multiple strands...

Be more rope.

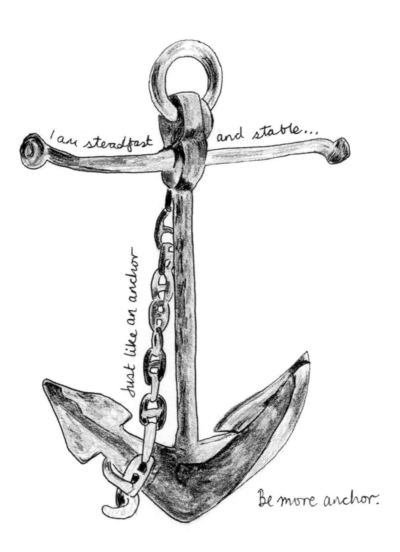

I am steadfast and stable...

just like an anchor

Be more anchor.

I can unlock my happiness...

that like a key

JOY HOPE FAITH TRUTH PEACE LOVE

Be more key.

Just like a palm tree

I am flexible in a storm...

Be more palm tree.

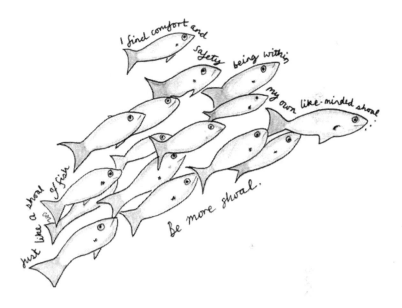

I find comfort and safety being within my own like-minded shoal.

just like a shoal of fish

Be more shoal.

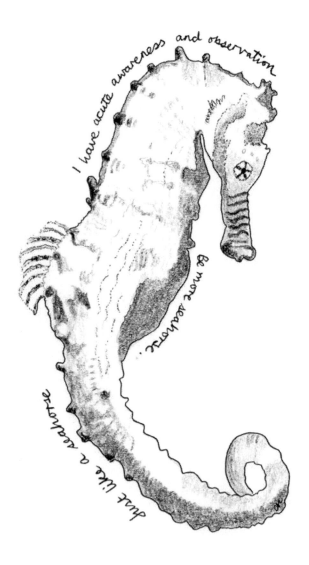

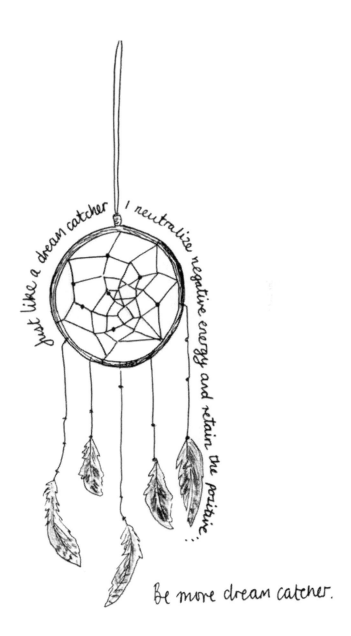

just like a dream catcher I neutralize negative energy and retain the positive...

Be more dream catcher.

just like a snowflake

embrace your uniqueness…

Be more snowflake.

Just like the word

amAZing,

I have an A-Z of
greatness within me...

Be more amAZing.

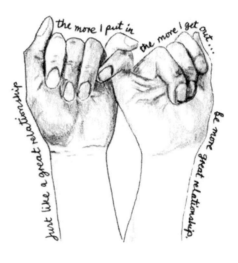

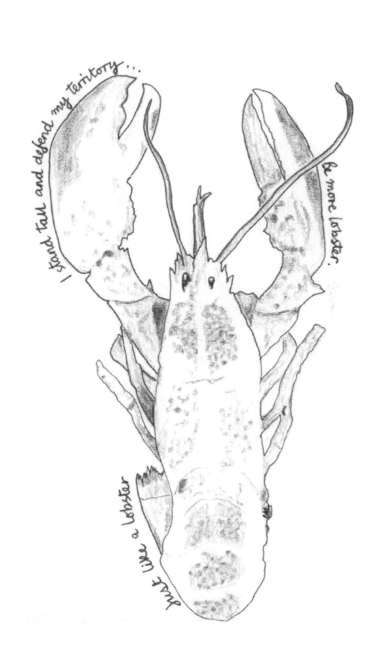

I stand tall and defend my territory...

be more lobster.

just like a lobster

Just like a runner. Keep moving forward... Be more runner.

The journey is the destination...

just like a pilgrim

Be more pilgrim.

Thanks

Thank you to Devra Jacobs at Dancing World Group, John Hunt Publishers who saw something in a completely unknown author and artist and trusted me in my mission. Thank you to my parents who support me wholeheartedly in all that I choose to do and to my dear friends who cheer me on all the way. Thank you to David Knight who introduced me to Chad E. Cooper who has inspired me to live a life with only the limitations I choose to place upon myself. Thank you to Oprah Winfrey whose amazing podcast interviews have inspired and challenged me as I ran mile after mile in the Suffolk countryside. Thank you to Dr Edith Egers for her book *The Choice* which changed my life, and finally thank you to my art teacher at Purcell School, Phil Barrett, who said in my sixth form leaving wishes "... I still think you'd have been better off doing art" ... Mr Barrett, better late than never...

Clare Langan, 26th October 2020

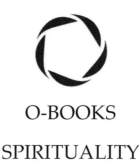

O-BOOKS

SPIRITUALITY

O is a symbol of the world, of oneness and unity; this eye represents knowledge and insight. We publish titles on general spirituality and living a spiritual life. We aim to inform and help you on your own journey in this life. If you have enjoyed this book, why not tell other readers by posting a review on your preferred book site?

Recent bestsellers from O-Books are:

Heart of Tantric Sex
Diana Richardson
Revealing Eastern secrets of deep love and intimacy to Western couples.
Paperback: 978-1-90381-637-0 ebook: 978-1-84694-637-0

Crystal Prescriptions
The A-Z guide to over 1,200 symptoms and their healing crystals
Judy Hall
The first in the popular series of eight books, this handy little guide is packed as tight as a pill-bottle with crystal remedies for ailments.
Paperback: 978-1-90504-740-6 ebook: 978-1-84694-629-5

Your Simple Path
Find Happiness in every step
Ian Tucker
A guide to helping us reconnect with what is really important in
our lives.
Paperback: 978-1-78279-349-6 ebook: 978-1-78279-348-9

365 Days of Wisdom
Daily Messages To Inspire You Through The Year
Dadi Janki
Daily messages which cool the mind, warm the heart and guide
you along your journey.
Paperback: 978-1-84694-863-3 ebook: 978-1-84694-864-0

Body of Wisdom
Women's Spiritual Power and How it Serves
Hilary Hart
Bringing together the dreams and experiences of women across
the world with today's most visionary spiritual teachers.
Paperback: 978-1-78099-696-7 ebook: 978-1-78099-695-0

Dying to Be Free
From Enforced Secrecy to Near Death to True Transformation
Hannah Robinson
After an unexpected accident and near-death experience, Hannah
Robinson found herself radically transforming her life, while a
remarkable new insight altered her relationship with her father, a
practising Catholic priest.
Paperback: 978-1-78535-254-6 ebook: 978-1-78535-255-3

The Ecology of the Soul
A Manual of Peace, Power and Personal Growth for Real People
in the Real World
Aidan Walker
Balance your own inner Ecology of the Soul to regain your
natural state of peace, power and wellbeing.
Paperback: 978-1-78279-850-7 ebook: 978-1-78279-849-1

Not I, Not other than I
The Life and Teachings of Russel Williams
Steve Taylor, Russel Williams
The miraculous life and inspiring teachings of one of the World's
greatest living Sages.
Paperback: 978-1-78279-729-6 ebook: 978-1-78279-728-9

On the Other Side of Love
A woman's unconventional journey towards wisdom
Muriel Maufroy
When life has lost all meaning, what do you do?
Paperback: 978-1-78535-281-2 ebook: 978-1-78535-282-9

Practicing A Course In Miracles
A translation of the Workbook in plain language, with
mentor's notes
Elizabeth A. Cronkhite
The practical second and third volumes of The Plain-Language
A Course In Miracles.
Paperback: 978-1-84694-403-1 ebook: 978-1-78099-072-9

Quantum Bliss
The Quantum Mechanics of Happiness, Abundance, and Health
George S. Mentz
Quantum Bliss is the breakthrough summary of success and
spirituality secrets that customers have been waiting for.
Paperback: 978-1-78535-203-4 ebook: 978-1-78535-204-1

The Upside Down Mountain
Mags MacKean
A must-read for anyone weary of chasing success and happiness
– one woman's inspirational journey swapping the uphill slog for
the downhill slope.
Paperback: 978-1-78535-171-6 ebook: 978-1-78535-172-3

Your Personal Tuning Fork
The Endocrine System
Deborah Bates
Discover your body's health secret, the endocrine system, and
'twang' your way to sustainable health!
Paperback: 978-1-84694-503-8 ebook: 978-1-78099-697-4

Readers of ebooks can buy or view any of these bestsellers by
clicking on the live link in the title. Most titles are published
in paperback and as an ebook. Paperbacks are available in
traditional bookshops. Both print and ebook formats are
available online.
Find more titles and sign up to our readers' newsletter at
http://www.johnhuntpublishing.com/mind-body-spirit
Follow us on Facebook at https://www.facebook.com/OBooks/
and Twitter at https://twitter.com/obooks